Mobile Addiction

21 Simple Techniques

To

Remove or Reduce

Mobile Addiction

In

Children/ Students and Adults

by
Internationally Renowned Author Couple

Abhishaik Chitraans
Rainu Mangtani

(ईष्ट कृपा एवं गुरु आशीष)

वसुदेवसुतं देवं कंसचाणूरमर्दनम्।
देवकीपरमानन्दं कृष्णं वन्दे जगद्गुरुम्॥

|| प्रार्थना ||

ॐ असतो मा सद्गमय
तमसो मा ज्योतिर्गमय
मृत्योर्मा अमृतं गमय
|| ॐ शान्तिः शान्तिः शान्तिः ||

Book Credits:

Book Title – Abhishaik Chitraans
Design Concept – Abhishaik Chitraans & Rainu Mangtani
Cover and Inside Images – Pixabay, Freepik
Cover Designed by – Stella Mary

Foreword Credits:

Abhijit Kumar
Director, Chitransh Academy,

Dr Navjot Kaur
Educationist and Mrs India Planet, 2022

Suudakshina Roy Deluca
School Personnel, Hove City Council Schools,
Brighton, U.K

The Institute of Occult Sciences, Spiritual Activities and Research
Regd. by Ministry of MSME, Govt. of India
ISO 9001:2015 Certified
IVAF & AAA (USA) Recognized

IVAF : International Vedic Astrology Federation (USA)
(An American Organization of Research)

AAA : Astrological Academic Alliances (USA)
(The World's Best International Astrology Forum

E-mail : ankakshrmiracless@gmail.com

Disclaimer

This book, **Mobile Addiction** (*21 Simple Techniques to Remove or Reduce Mobile Addiction in Children/ Students and Adults*), is intended to provide general information and guidance on managing mobile addiction. It is not a substitute for professional medical, psychological or therapeutic advice. Readers are encouraged to consult a qualified professional or healthcare provider for personalized guidance, particularly if they or their loved ones experience significant challenges related to addiction, mental health or behaviour.

The techniques, advice and suggestions provided in this book are based on the authors' research and experiences. Individual results may vary and the effectiveness of these techniques may depend on each person's unique circumstances. The authors and publisher disclaim any liability for loss, injury or damage incurred as a result of the use of information provided in this book.

|| ॐ ||

Contents

Heartiest Greetings!

Respected Parents/ Teachers and Dear Students, as this is very critical situation at present about **'Mobile'** phone, No one can imagine the world without mobile. We already know that our mobile can solve every task which comes in our mind. Everyone thinks that mobile can handle all the problems, which comes in the mind, including social media and current news, meaning searching, distance check, photos and image searching and whatever.

The use of mobile devices can have both **'Positive & Negative'** impacts on school students. For the school students, project working, holiday homework, English to Hindi meaning search, English to English search, topic search and many more. So, school life has become very easy with the help of one mobile phone only.

It's important to note that while mobile devices offer these advantages, there are potential drawbacks as well. Excessive screen time, distraction and access to non-educational content are concerns that need to be addressed. Schools and Parents should collaborate to set clear guidelines for responsible mobile device usage, including appropriate times for usage, content restrictions and balance between screen time and other activities.

Ultimately, the use of mobile devices in education should be guided by a thoughtful and balanced approach that takes into consideration the specific needs of the students and the educational goals of the school.

This is the most common problem in today's scenario because each family/ parents/ teachers/ doctors/ psychologists are disturb due to *"Mobile Addiction in Children/ Students and Adults"* and no one in the family as strict, who can stop this.

We can't remove the mobile phone from your hands, because of its importance, but can handle it's time limit for maintaining the health as well as our child's future.

Certainly, 21 simple, but important techniques to remove or reduce **"Mobile Addiction in Children/ Students/ Adults"**, are shared in next chapters.

Dedication

This book is dedicated to all those who are seeking to regain control in a world increasingly dominated by mobile devices. To the children, parents, teachers and adults, who recognize the importance of balance and wish to break free from the grips of **'Mobile Addiction'**, may these 21 techniques empower you to reclaim your time, well-being and relationships.

Dedicate this work to the unwavering spirit of self-awareness and self-improvement that drives each of us toward healthier digital habits. A special thanks to our family, friends, mentors and every individual, who has contributed their insights and experiences to this journey reducing as well as removing the **Mobile Addiction.**

|| ॐ ||

Acknowledgement

We would like to extend my heartfelt gratitude to all those, who have supported and guided me in the creation of this book. First and foremost, my deepest thanks to our family and friends for their unwavering love, understanding and encouragement throughout this journey. Their support has been the pillar of strength.

To Abhijit Kumar, Director of **'Chitransh Academy'**, for his continuous inspiration and invaluable insights that helped shape the foundation of this work.

We also want to express our appreciation to the many experts, educators, psychologists and parents, who shared their experiences and knowledge with us. Your contributions have been instrumental in crafting practical techniques for managing and reducing the addiction.

To our friends, colleagues and readers – thank you for your trust and support. It is your belief in this book that has driven us to ensure it reaches as many individuals as possible, helping them take the necessary steps toward a more balanced life.

Finally, to all the children/ students and adults, who are struggling with mobile addiction, this book is for you. May it offer the tools, inspiration and hope to transform your relationship with technology for the better health and bright future.

Best Wishes and Regards,
Abhishaik & Rainu

Foreword by Abhijit Kumar

Abhijit Kumar

M.A., B.Ed., M.B.A., L.L.B.

Director, Chitransh Academy

Bareilly, (U.P) India

In an age, where technology touches every aspect of our lives, mobile devices have become indispensable yet sometimes overwhelming companions. While their convenience and connectivity are undeniable, the growing dependency on mobile phones is affecting individuals and families on a deeper level. Mobile addiction, especially among children and adults, is quietly reshaping attention spans, relationships and mental well-being. This book, **'Mobile Addiction'** : *21 Simple Techniques to Remove or Reduce Mobile Addiction in Children/ Students and Adults,* addresses these pressing concerns with practical and thoughtful solutions.

As the Director of **'Chitransh Academy'**, I have witnessed first-hand the impact of 'mobile addiction' on students and families alike. Parents, teachers and communities grapple with how best to help the next generation develop a healthy relationship with technology. This book offers a refreshingly realistic approach, combining insight with actionable strategies that readers can implement immediately. It emphasizes moderation and conscious use rather than imposing strict restrictions, making it suitable for a wide audience seeking to regain control over their digital habits.

The authors' methods are straightforward yet impactful, crafted with an understanding of modern challenges. This guide is a valuable resource for anyone looking to improve focus, build stronger connections and foster a balanced lifestyle in today's tech-driven world. It stands out as a guiding light for families, educators and individuals, who aim to empower them-selves and others in overcoming the pitfalls of mobile overuse.

I am pleased to present this timely work, which will undoubtedly inspire readers to take positive steps toward healthier mobile habits. I hope you find it as enlightening and empowering as I have.

Abhijit Kumar
Director, Chitransh Academy
Bareilly (U.P)

Abhijit Kumar is a distinguished educationist with a rich academic background, holding degrees in Mathematics, Economics (M.A.), B.Ed., M.B.A. and L.L.B. With experience in various esteemed institutions and companies, he has been managing his own Computer Institute and a franchise of distance learning centre for Deemed Universities' distance learning courses since 1999. A young management professional, he embodies the spirit of today's technical generation, bringing a modern perspective to education and professional development with good and healthy environment.

Foreword by Dr Navjot Kaur

Dr. Navjot Kaur
Educationist, Director of Administration,
Author, Entrepreneur and Mrs. India Planet 2022
Punjab, India

In an era where technology is omnipresent, our lives have become intertwined with the screens of our mobile devices. The evolution of mobile technology has undeniably brought convenience, connectivity and information to our fingertips. Yet, as with any powerful tool, it has also led to unforeseen consequences. Mobile addiction is now a serious concern, subtly but profoundly influencing our lives, our relationships and even our mental well-being.

Today, a significant percentage of people spend hours scrolling through endless streams of content, often without realizing the time slipping away. Social media platforms, gaming apps and constant notifications have created a digital trap, luring individuals into a state of dependency. As we become engrossed in the virtual world, our real-world connections and personal productivity suffers. This is especially concerning for younger generations who are growing up in an environment where mobile devices are constant companions, potentially affecting their growth, learning and personal development.

This book by **Mr. Abhishaik Chitraans** and **Mrs. Rainu Mangtani** is a profound initiative addressing this pressing issue. Through insightful research, real-life stories and actionable advice, the authors shed light on the psychological impact of mobile addiction and offer readers the tools they need to reclaim control over their lives. This is not merely a book about technology; it is a powerful reminder of the importance of balance in our digital world.

As an educationist and a beauty queen (Mrs. India Planet 2022), I have had the privilege of engaging with diverse audiences, young minds and raising awareness on various social issues. I have encountered many young people undergoing therapeutic interventions to achieve a digital detox. It's becoming increasingly common among the younger generation, highlighting the widespread impact of digital overload. I have witnessed first-hand how pervasive mobile addiction has become, often as a result of unconscious behaviour patterns that are difficult to break. It is my belief that books like this serve as an phenomenal guide, helping us navigate the challenges posed by technology while making informed choices about our digital consumption.

As you turn the pages of this book, I invite you to reflect on your own relationship with your mobile devices. Recognize the potential for growth and productivity that lies beyond the screens and allow yourself to reconnect with the world around you. Mr. and Mrs. Chitraans have crafted a valuable resource that will inspire you to seek balance, prioritize personal connections and foster a healthier approach to technology. May this book ignite awareness and empower you to break free from the chains of mobile addiction, embracing a life of purpose, mindfulness and true connections.

Dr. Navjot Kaur
Punjab

Dr. Navjot Kaur, is a young dynamic educationist. She is a Director of Administration of an eminent educational institution and an active member of the Advisory Board to schools. Adorning several crowns, she is a true beauty with purpose, an educationist by profession with the fundamental aim to enlighten several lives. She believes in imparting right knowledge and encouraging women to believe in their dreams and unleash one's true potential.

She received numerous international and national accolades and awards for exemplary leadership skills in the field of education. She is a woman with power and positive influence, who exudes unprecedented strength and valour with optimistic outlook to face all challenges of life tenaciously.

Dr Navjot Kaur is a truly epitome of beauty with brain as winning the national title of Mrs. India Planet 2022. She proved to be an inspiration and encouragement to ample of women to believe in themselves and vanquish greatness in life. With a vibrant blend of grace, intellect and dedication, She has made her mark, embodying the true spirit of an empowered and inspirational woman.

Foreword by Suudakshina Roy Deluca

Suudakshina Roy Deluca,
School Personnel, Hove City Council Schools,
Brighton, United Kingdom

As school personnel, working for Brighton and Hove city council schools in United Kingdom, I have witnessed first-hand the growing influence of mobile technology on children's lives. While innovation connects us to endless possibilities, it also poses unique challenges, especially in shaping young minds.

'Mobile Addiction' : *21 Simple Techniques to Remove or Reduce Mobile Addiction in Children/ Students and Adults* is a timely guide that addresses this modern dilemma with practical and thoughtful solutions. This book goes beyond criticism and offers a pathway to balance—a balance crucial for nurturing creativity, focus and well-being in both children and adults.

In a world dominated by screens, this work reminds us of the importance of reclaiming human connections and cherishing the moments that truly matter. It is a must-read book for educators, parents and students as well or anyone looking to foster a healthier relationship with technology by minimum or necessary usage only.

Suudakshina Roy Deluca,
School Personnel, Hove City Council Schools,
Brighton, United Kingdom

Suudakshina Roy Deluca is a qualified and multitalented international educationist. She has done M.Sc. in Environmental Science from Pune University, simultaneously M.Phil. & Post Graduation Certificate of Education (PGCE) from Sussex University, U.K.

She is too courageous and self-dependent lady, love to make new friends and spend the time with kids, students and family friends. She is an avid traveller and having keen interest to know the psychology and opinion of different people about life. She is responsible and lovable mother of two.

Suudakshina has deep interest in Occult Sciences i.e. Numerology and Astrology etc.

Abhishaik Chitraans (Author)

Abhishaik Chitraans
M.Com., M.A., M.B.A.
Certified Master Numerologist and Consultant, IVAF & AAA (USA)

Abhishaik Chitraans is a distinguished numerologist, educator and internationally renowned published author, poet, expert columnist, philosopher as well as the visionary Founder and CEO of **Ankakshr Miracless,** *The Institute of Occult Sciences, Spiritual Activities and Research,* an institution registered by the Ministry of MSME, Government of India and Certified with ISO 9001:1015. Recognized by IVAF (International Vedic Astrology Federation) & AAA (Astrological Academic Alliances), USA. *Ankakshr Miracless* stands as a testament to Abhishaik's commitment to advancing numerology on a global scale. He is celebrated as the only numerologist worldwide to develop over five unique numerological formulas, combining the principles of BODMAS (mathematics) and physics to calculate life paths through date of birth. His contributions have set a new standard in numerology and his research has been published in over 10 international journals and prominent astrological magazines, including presentations at UGC-approved universities.

With three master's degrees in Commerce (M.Com.), Economics (M.A.) and Business Administration (MBA), Abhishaik brings a profound understanding of both academia and practical expertise. His professional journey spans more than a decade in high-level finance roles, including as Deputy General Manager of Accounts, Banking & Finance and an Internal Auditor with a top-10-ranked shipping cargo company in Africa and the Gulf region. However, his career took a remarkable turn in 2009, when he was diagnosed with *'Transverse Myelitis'*, an untreatable condition that has left his lower limbs paralyzed. Despite this, he continues to excel and inspire, earning the moniker **'The Bed Traveller'** for his resilience and dedication to his life's mission.

In addition to his professional achievements, Abhishaik has become a Certified Professional Teacher, with a significant educational impact. He has guided over 1,000 Students/ Clients across 10+ countries, offering insights and consultations in numerology that span the globe. His published works include more than 30 articles on numerology and name numerology across leading magazines and online platforms.

Abhishaik's excellence and dedication have been widely recognized with numerous awards:

- World Record Holder for an International Poetry Anthology on Zodiac Signs
- First Prize in a state-level article writing competition by PCRA in Uttar Pradesh
- Excellence in Numerology & Research by ISA

- Jyotish Gaurav, Astro Diamond, Manavta Ratn, Vishisht Hindi Sewi, Sahitya Alankar Samman, Thai Sri Buddha Maharshi Award and Maharshi Agasthya Award etc.

Abhishaik Chitraans exemplifies resilience, knowledge and global influence in numerology, continually enriching the field with ground-breaking insights, innovative methodologies and a passion for transforming lives.

Rainu Mangtani (Author)

Rainu Mangtani
M.Com., IIBF Certified Digital Banker
Certified Numerologist and Graphologist

Rainu Mangtani, celebrated as *'The Versatile Iconic Personality',* is a distinguished figure whose accomplishments span diverse fields, including banking, literature, content creation and motivational speaking. A certified numerologist and graphologist with M.Com and IIBF Certification as a Digital Banker, Rainu has over six years of experience in the banking and insurance sectors, specializing in digital products for international clients and NRIs. Her professional expertise is matched by her impressive literary journey as a self-published and internationally recognized author, co-authored over 25 books and compiled six anthologies that have highlighted over 500 voices.

Renowned for her dynamic presence, Rainu has graced multiple magazine covers, establishing herself as a true icon. She has been awarded titles such as *'Youth Icon'* by the Governor of Maharashtra and Asia's Top 30 Leading Women. She is an Expert Columnist, Best Author of the year 2022, Model Icon, Social Activist, World Record Holder, Perfect Author of year 2022, Best Content Writer of year 2023, Vlogger, The Celebrity Queen, Brand Ambassador, Crown Girl, Speaker: Swell cast (Voice Over Artist). She's also the recipient of the prestigious National & International Dr APJ Abdul Kalam Awardee and got participation certificate for contributing her story to the world of cinema. As a finalist for CT Miss India International 2022, adding another dimension to her impressive repertoire recognized as *'The Celebrity Queen'*, a model and an inspirational figure.

Her works, *The Height of Life in 24 Rains*, *Today's Corporate World (A Robotic Mechanism of Youth)* and *Ladder of Success*, reflect her commitment to inspiring others.

In addition to her books Rainu Mangtani has also compiled and contributed to **Women Empowerment and Economic Developments,** an anthology with 51 co-authors launched on International Women's Day and Mahashivratri (March 8, 2024), where Padma Shri recipient Smt. Gulabo Sapera served as the Chief Guest. Currently, She is working on *'My Marriage : Bliss vs Curse'* and *'Seven LEE of Life'*, the anthology books that includes contributions from 108 visionary co-authors, delving into the complex experiences of marriage and abundance of life resp.

Rainu Mangtani is also a celebrated podcaster on **Ankakshr Miracless'** YouTube channel, a vlogger and an influential voice in the content creation realm. She uses this platform for empowerment and change, making her a beloved figure and an enduring *'Crown Girl'* in the public eyes.

By
Internationally Renowned Author Couple

Abhishaik Chitraans
Rainu Mangtani

(ईष्ट कृपा एवं गुरु आशीष)

01

Set Screen Time Limits

Establish clear limits on the amount of time children can spend on their mobile devices each day. Use parental control apps or device settings to enforce these limits.

Setting screen time limits is an effective strategy to help students manage and reduce mobile device addiction.

a). **Assess Current Usage**: Start by understanding how much time the student currently spends on their mobile device. This will give you a baseline to work from.

b). **Choose Realistic Limits**: Set realistic and age-appropriate limits on daily screen time. Guidelines vary, but the American Academy of Pediatrics, for instance, recommends no more than 1 to 2 hours of recreational screen time per day for school-age children.

c). **Set Specific Time Windows**: Define specific time windows during which the student is allowed to use their mobile device. For example, you might designate a certain period after school hours or during weekends.

d). **Involve the Student**: Discuss the importance of balanced screen time with the student. Explain the potential negative impacts of excessive screen time on health, sleep and academic performance. Involve them in the process of setting their own limits to increase their sense of responsibility.

e). **Prioritize Offline Activities**: Encourage the student to engage in offline activities that they enjoy, such as sports, reading, arts and crafts or spending time with family and friends. This reduces their reliance on screens for entertainment.

f). **Use Parental Control Apps**: Utilize parental control apps or built-in device features to enforce screen time limits. These tools allow you to set time restrictions, track usage and even remotely manage devices.

g). **Implement Device-Free Zones**: Designate certain areas or times as device-free zones, such as during family meals or in bedrooms before bedtime. This promotes healthy habits and better sleep.

h). **Monitor Progress**: Regularly review the student's screen time usage and progress. Make adjustments to the limits if necessary, considering their academic workload and extracurricular commitments.

i). **Create a Schedule**: Create a daily schedule that includes time for homework, physical activity, hobbies, social interactions and screen time. Having a structured routine helps students manage their time effectively.

j). **Provide Alternatives**: Offer alternative activities that students can engage in when they're not using their mobile devices. Having a variety of options can make it easier for them to shift their focus away from screens.

k). **Lead by Example**: Model responsible screen time behavior yourself. Children are more likely to follow guidelines when they see adults adhering to them as well.

l). **Reward Responsible Usage**: Offer positive reinforcement when the student adheres to the screen time limits. This could involve extra privileges, rewards or simply acknowledging their efforts.

Remember that while setting screen time limits is important, it's also essential to maintain open communication with the student/ children. Discuss the reasons behind the limits, address any concerns they might have and listen to their feedback. The goal is to create a healthy balance between screen time and other important activities in their lives.

|| ॐ ||

02

Create Tech-Free Zones

Designate certain areas of the house, such as the dining room or bedrooms, as tech-free zones where mobile devices are not allowed. This encourages face-to-face interactions and healthier habits.

Creating tech-free zones is a great strategy to reduce mobile device addiction and promote healthier habits. These zones provide designated areas where individuals, especially students can disconnect from their devices and focus on other activities. Here's how you can create effective tech-free zones:

a). **Identify Key Areas**: Determine which areas of your home or school should be designated as tech-free zones. Common areas could include bedrooms, dining areas, study spaces and certain recreational spaces.

b). **Set Clear Boundaries**: Clearly define the boundaries of the tech-free zones using visual cues or signage. This helps establish a physical reminder that these areas are meant for disconnecting from devices.

c). **Communicate the Purpose**: Explain to family members or students the purpose behind creating tech-free zones. Emphasize the importance of face-to-face interactions, relaxation and focusing on non-screen activities.

d). **Enforce Consistency**: Consistency is the key to making tech-free zones effective. Ensure that everyone understands and respects the boundaries at all times, including guests or visitors.

e). **Design Comfortable Spaces**: Make tech-free zones inviting by creating comfortable seating arrangements, providing soft lighting and incorporating elements that encourage relaxation and social interaction.

f). **Establish Screen-Free Times**: In addition to physical spaces, consider designating specific times of the day when devices are not allowed in these zones, such as during meals or before bedtime.

g). **Provide Alternative Activities**: Fill tech-free zones with alternative activities that don't involve screens. This could include books, puzzles, board games, musical instruments or art supplies.

h). **Educate About Benefits**: Discuss the benefits of disconnecting from screens in tech-free zones, such as improved sleep quality, better communication and reduced digital distractions.

i). **Lead by Example**: Adults and authority figures should model the behavior they expect from others. Demonstrate responsible device usage by adhering to tech-free zone guidelines yourself.

j). **Create Family or Community Agreements**: Develop agreements or guidelines as a family or community that outline the rules and expectations for using devices within the designated tech-free zones.

k). **Encourage Interaction**: Plan activities that encourage interaction and bonding within these zones. Family discussions, game nights, storytelling or simply spending quality time together can strengthen relationships.

1). **Regularly Evaluate and Adjust**: Periodically review the effectiveness of the tech-free zones and make adjustments if needed. Solicit feedback from family members, students or participants to ensure the zones meet their needs.

Remember that the goal of creating tech-free zones is not to completely eliminate screen time but to strike a balance between screen-related activities and other valuable experiences. By establishing these zones and fostering a positive environment within them, you can help individuals break away from the habit of constant device use and encourage healthier lifestyle choices.

|| ॐ ||

03

Engage in Outdoor Activities

Encourage children to participate in outdoor activities, sports and hobbies that don't involve mobile devices. Spending time outdoors can help reduce reliance on screens.

Engaging in outdoor activities is a fantastic way to reduce mobile device addiction, promote physical and mental well-being and encourage a more balanced lifestyle. Here are some outdoor activities that can help individuals, especially students, disconnect from screens and enjoy the outdoors:

a). **Hiking and Nature Walks**: Explore local trails, nature reserves or parks. Hiking not only provides exercise but also allows for peaceful contemplation and connection with nature.

b). **Cycling or Rollerblading**: Ride bicycles or rollerblades around the neighborhood, in parks or on dedicated paths. It's a fun way to stay active and enjoy the outdoors.

c). **Sports and Team Games**: Organize or join friendly sports matches such as soccer, basketball or volleyball. Team sports encourage interaction and physical activity.

d). **Picnics and Outdoor Meals**: Plan picnics in parks or open spaces. Bring along healthy snacks and meals to enjoy while soaking in the fresh air.

e). **Gardening**: Cultivate a garden at home or participate in community gardening projects. Gardening offers a productive and therapeutic way to spend time outdoors.

f). **Nature Photography**: Encourage individuals to capture the beauty of the outdoors through photography. This activity combines creativity with exploration.

g). **Stargazing**: Spend evenings stargazing and observing celestial phenomena. This can be a tranquil and educational experience.

h). **Dog Walking**: If you have a pet dog, taking them for regular walks is not only beneficial for their health but also encourages you to get outdoors.

i). **Outdoor Yoga or Meditation**: Practice yoga or meditation in natural settings. The outdoors can provide a serene backdrop for relaxation and mindfulness.

j). **Art and Craft Activities**: Set up an outdoor art station for drawing, painting or crafting. Nature can serve as inspiration for creative projects.

k). **Beach Trips or Water Activities**: If you're near a beach, lake or river, consider swimming, kayaking, paddle boarding or simply enjoying the water and sun.

Remember, the goal is to disconnect from screens and immerse oneself in the physical world. Encourage friends, family or fellow students to participate in these activities together, fostering social interaction and positive experiences. Prioritize safety by adhering to any local guidelines or restrictions related to outdoor activities. By incorporating these outdoor activities into your routine, you can help break the cycle of mobile device addiction and enjoy the many benefits of spending time in nature.

|| ॐ ||

Provide Alternative Entertainment

Offer alternative forms of entertainment such as books, puzzles, board games or art and craft activities. Engaging in these activities can divert children's attention from screens.

Offering alternative forms of entertainment can be a great way to help individuals, especially students, reduce mobile device addiction and engage in more balanced activities. Here are some ideas for alternative entertainment options:

a). **Books and Reading**: Encourage reading by providing a variety of books that cater to different interests and reading levels. Whether fiction, non-fiction or comics, reading can captivate and engage the mind.

b). **Board Games and Puzzles**: Gather family or friends for board games or puzzles that require strategic thinking, problem-solving and social interaction.

c). **Art and Craft Projects**: Provide art supplies for drawing, painting, crafting or DIY projects. Creative activities stimulate imagination and offer a hands-on outlet for self-expression.

d). **Musical Instruments**: If there's an interest in music, consider learning to play a musical instrument. It's a rewarding way to spend time and develop a new skill.

e). **Cooking and Baking**: Experiment with cooking or baking new recipes. This not only engages the senses but also offers the satisfaction of creating something delicious.

f). **Outdoor Sports and Activities**: Engage in sports like basketball, soccer, tennis etc.. Outdoor activities promote physical fitness and social bonding.

g). **Indoor Exercise**: Offer workout routines or yoga sessions that can be done indoors. There are plenty of online resources available for guided workouts.

h). **Listening to Music or Podcasts**: Explore different genres of music or listen to educational and entertaining podcasts. It's a way to engage the mind without relying on screens.

i). **Journaling or Writing**: Encourage keeping a journal, writing short stories or even trying poetry. Writing can be a creative outlet for self-reflection and expression.

j). **Photography**: Promote photography as a way to capture moments and express creativity. This can be done using a digital camera or even a smart phone.

k). **Explore Nature**: Spend time outdoors by hiking, bird watching, stargazing or exploring local parks. Nature offers a refreshing break from screens.

l). **Volunteer Activities**: Engage in volunteer work or community service. Contributing to the community can be fulfilling and create a sense of purpose.

m). **Learning New Skills**: Encourage the pursuit of new skills or hobbies, whether it's cooking, coding, painting, knitting or anything else that piques interest.

n). **Socializing and Conversations**: Spend quality time with friends and family through meaningful conversations, game nights or simply bonding over shared experiences.

By offering a diverse range of alternative entertainment options, you can help individuals find activities that captivate their interests, challenge their minds and provide a sense of fulfillment. The key is to make these activities accessible, enjoyable and part of a healthy and balanced lifestyle.

|| ॐ ||

05

Establish Screen-Free Times

Designate specific times of the day as "screen-free," such as during meals, before bedtime or when doing homework. This promotes healthy routines and quality family time.

Establishing screen-free times is an effective strategy to reduce mobile device addiction and create a healthier balance between screen time and other activities. Here's how you can set up screen-free times:

a). **Identify Key Time Periods**: Determine specific time periods during the day when screens will be off-limits. These periods could include meal times, before bedtime or designated family hours.

b). **Communicate the Plan**: Clearly communicate the screen-free times to all family members, roommates or individuals involved. Make sure everyone is aware of the schedule and its importance.

c). **Lead by Example**: Adults and authority figures should be the role models for adhering to screen-free times. Demonstrate the behavior you expect from others.

d). **Use Technology**: Utilize technology to your advantage. Set device alarms or notifications to remind everyone when screen-free times are about to start.

e). **Create a Charging Station**: Designate a central charging station outside of bedrooms where devices are placed during screen-free times. This prevents the temptation to use devices late at night.

f). **Engage in Alternative Activities**: During screen-free times, engage in alternative activities such as reading, playing board games, having conversations or participating in hobbies.

g). **Encourage Outdoor Time**: Allocate screen-free times for outdoor activities like walks, picnics, gardening or simply enjoying nature.

h). **Unplug Before Bed**: Establish a screen-free period before bedtime to promote better sleep quality. The blue light emitted by screens can interfere with sleep patterns.

i). **Family or Group Activities**: Plan regular family or group activities during screen-free times to encourage bonding and social interaction.

j). **Reflect and Evaluate**: After implementing screen-free times, periodically reflect on how they're impacting your daily routine and family dynamics. Make adjustments if needed.

k). **Use a Family Agreement**: Develop a family agreement or set of guidelines that outline the rules and expectations for screen-free times. Involve all members in the decision-making process.

l). **Reward Positive Behavior**: Recognize and reward adherence to screen-free times. This could involve simple acknowledgments, special privileges or small treats.

m). **Review and Adjust**: Regularly review the effectiveness of the screen-free times and make adjustments based on feedback and observations.

Remember that the goal of establishing screen-free times is not only to reduce device addiction but also to promote healthier habits, improve communication and create opportunities for meaningful experiences. By setting clear boundaries and encouraging engaging activities during these periods, you can help individuals break away from constant screen use and lead a more balanced lifestyle.

|| ॐ ||

06

Encourage Social Interaction

Encourage children to interact with friends and family members in person rather than solely through digital communication. Plan playing dates, outings or gatherings to facilitate social interactions.

Encouraging social interaction is a powerful way to reduce mobile device addiction and create more meaningful connections with others. Here are several strategies to promote social interaction:

a). **Family or Friend Gatherings**: Organize regular family or friend gatherings where everyone can engage in face-to-face conversations, games or shared activities.

b). **Designated Social Hours**: Set specific hours during the day when everyone is encouraged to put away their devices and engage in quality social interactions.

c). **Tech-Free Meals**: Make meal time tech-free zones, where everyone sits down together, shares a meal and enjoys conversation without distractions.

d). **Group Activities**: Plan group activities that require interaction, such as game nights, movie marathons or outdoor outings.

e). **Community Involvement**: Encourage participation in community events, clubs or volunteer activities that foster interactions with others.

f). **Shared Hobbies**: Identify shared hobbies or interests among family members or friends and dedicate time to engaging in these activities together.

g). **Sports and Fitness Classes**: Joining sports teams, fitness classes or group exercise sessions can provide opportunities for socializing while staying active.

h). **Creative Workshops**: Attend workshops or classes that involve creative activities like painting, cooking, dancing or crafting. These classes offer a chance to meet new people and learn new skills.

i). **Family Game Nights**: Dedicate a regular evening to playing board games, card games or interactive video games that encourage friendly competition and bonding.

j). **Outdoor Adventures**: Plan outdoor adventures like hiking, picnics or sports that bring people together in a natural setting.

k). **Technology-Free Zones**: Create designated technology-free zones or times where everyone commits to being present and engaged with each other.

l). **Phone Stacking**: During social gatherings, have everyone stack their phones in a designated area. This encourages participants to focus on the present moment and each other.

m). **Group Chats and Calls**: Utilize group chats and video calls to stay connected with friends and family members, who may be physically distant.

n). **Networking Events**: Attend networking events, workshops or seminars related to personal or professional interests to expand social circles.

o). **Open Communication**: Keep communication lines open and encourage family members or friends to express their desire for more meaningful interactions.

p). **Practice Active Listening**: Encourage active listening during conversations, showing genuine interest in what others have to say.

q). **Plan Themed Parties**: Organize themed parties or gatherings that encourage creativity and socialization such as costume parties or potluck dinners.

Remember that genuine connections and interactions help combat feelings of isolation and loneliness that can contribute to mobile addiction. Creating opportunities for meaningful social engagement can improve overall well-being and make life more fulfilling.

|| ॐ ||

Set Up a Charging Station

Create a central charging station outside of bedrooms, where mobile devices are charged overnight. This prevents late-night device use and encourages better sleep hygiene.

Setting up a designated charging station is an effective strategy to help individuals, especially students, reduce mobile device addiction and establish healthier screen habits. Here's how you can create an effective charging station:

a). **Choose a Central Location**: Select a central and easily accessible location for the charging station. It could be in a common area like the living room, kitchen or study area.

b). **Use a Charging Organizer**: Invest in a charging organizer or station that can accommodate multiple devices. This keeps charging cables organized and prevents clutter.

c). **Designate a Specific Time**: Establish a specific time when individuals are required to place their devices on the charging station. This could be during designated screen-free times or before bedtime.

d). **Set Up Clear Guidelines**: Clearly communicate the rules and expectations for using the charging station. Explain the importance of disconnecting from devices during certain periods.

e). **Involve Everyone**: If it's a family or shared space, involve all family members or roommates in the decision to use the charging station. This creates a sense of accountability.

f). **Provide Alternative Activities**: Encourage individuals to engage in alternative activities during the times their devices are on the charging station. Offer options like reading, spending time with family or pursuing hobbies.

g). **Lead by Example**: Adults and authority figures should demonstrate the behavior they expect from others by also placing their devices on the charging station.

h). **Use Timers or Alarms**: Set timers or alarms on devices to remind individuals when it's time to place their devices on the charging station.

i). **Create a Tech-Free Zone**: Make the charging station area a tech-free zone during specific times. This encourages individuals to disconnect and engage in non-screen activities.

j). **Educate About the Benefits**: Explain the benefits of having designated screen-free times, such as improved sleep quality and enhanced face-to-face interactions.

k). **Gradual Implementation**: If complete disconnection seems challenging, start by implementing the charging station for a portion of the day and gradually increase the duration.

l). **Evaluate and Adjust**: Regularly assess the effectiveness of the charging station strategy. Gather feedback and make adjustments based on the progress observed.

m). **Reward Positive Behavior**: Recognize and reward individuals who consistently adhere to the charging station routine. This positive reinforcement reinforces the desired behavior.

n). **Personalize the Space**: Personalize the charging station area with motivational quotes, artwork or reminders of the benefits of reducing screen time.

Remember that the goal of the charging station is to create a designated space and time for disconnecting from devices and fostering healthier habits. By implementing this strategy and promoting responsible screen usage, you can contribute to a more balanced and mindful approach to technology.

‖ ॐ ‖

08

Involve in Art & Craft

Engaging in art and craft activities allows individuals to express themselves creatively. This shift in focus from screens to tangible materials stimulates the brain's creative centers, offering a satisfying alternative to digital entertainment. Children can explore their imagination through painting, drawing or crafting, which not only occupies their time but also fosters self-expression and individuality.

a). **Enhances Focus and Attention:** Art and craft require concentration and attention to detail. This practice can help individuals especially children develop their ability to focus on a single task without the constant distractions of notifications and digital stimuli. As they work on projects, they learn to immerse themselves in the present moment, reducing the urge to check their devices.

b). **Improves Fine Motor Skills:** Crafting activities such as cutting, gluing and painting enhance fine motor skills, particularly in young children. This development is crucial as it aids in overall cognitive growth and promotes physical coordination, encouraging an active engagement with the world around them rather than passively consuming content on screens.

c). **Builds Problem-Solving Skills:** Many art projects involve planning, decision-making and problem-solving. Whether it's figuring out how to structure a collage or selecting the right color for a painting, these activities challenge individuals to think critically and find solutions independently. This skill transfer can empower children and adults alike to tackle real-life challenges without relying on their devices for quick fixes.

d).   **Provides a Sense of Accomplishment:** Completing an art or craft project provides a tangible sense of accomplishment. This feeling can boost self-esteem and motivation, countering the often fleeting gratification from mobile device use. When children see their finished artwork or crafts, it reinforces the idea that they can create and achieve outside of digital environments.

e).   **Encourages Social Interaction:** Art and craft can be a communal activity that fosters social connections. Group projects or workshops encourage teamwork and collaboration, allowing participants to bond over shared experiences. This social interaction is essential in combating the loneliness and isolation that can come from excessive mobile usage, helping individuals to build stronger relationships in real life.

f).   **Reduces Stress and Anxiety:** Engaging in artistic activities has been shown to reduce stress and anxiety levels. The process of creating art can serve as a form of mindfulness, allowing individuals to focus on their feelings and express them creatively rather than through digital outlets. This therapeutic aspect of art can be especially beneficial for both children and adults looking to manage their emotions without turning to screens.

g).   **Promotes Mindfulness:** Art and craft activities encourage mindfulness by allowing individuals to immerse themselves fully in the creative process. This can help reduce the constant urge to check phones or engage with digital media, as individuals become more aware of their surroundings and the materials they are working with. Mindfulness in art can lead to a deeper appreciation of the present moment, diminishing the habitual impulse to seek distraction through mobile devices.

h). **Facilitates Learning Opportunities:** Art can be integrated into educational experiences, promoting learning across subjects like science, history and math. For example, creating a diorama can enhance understanding of ecological systems, while making a timeline can illustrate historical events. This interdisciplinary approach not only keeps children engaged but also reduces reliance on screens for educational content.

i). **Encourages Exploration of Interests:** Art and craft provide a platform for individuals to explore their interests and passions outside of the digital realm. Whether it's sculpting, knitting or digital art, engaging in creative activities helps individuals discover talents and hobbies that they may not have known about, fostering a sense of identity that is independent of mobile devices.

How to implement the above strategies:

1). **Art & Craft Workshops:** Organize community workshops for children and adults that focus on various art and craft techniques. This not only provides hands-on experiences but also promotes social interaction and teamwork.

2). **Set Up Craft Stations at Home:** Encourage families to set up dedicated spaces for arts and crafts in their homes, stocked with supplies that can entice both children and adults to engage in creative activities rather than reaching for their phones.

3). **Incorporate Art into Family Time:** Suggest families dedicate time to art activities during family nights, turning off devices to focus on creating together. This not only enhances family bonding but also establishes a routine that prioritizes creative engagement over digital consumption.

4). **Art Challenges:** Initiate art challenges, whether at home, in schools or online (in a limited capacity), where participants can showcase their work without the need for mobile devices. This can inspire creativity while reducing screen time.

5). **Competition:** Create an environment of competition to involve better with courage and creativity.

|| ॐ ||

09

Educational Games

Reducing mobile addiction, while keeping kids engaged with educational games is a common concern. The goal is to introduce children to games that encourage interaction with the real world, engage their hands and require creativity without heavy reliance on digital screens. Here are some educational games and activities that balance learning with a hands-on approach:

a). **Game Kits:** Encourage children to build and create, developing their spatial and fine motor skills. Many kits also include educational themes like robotics and STEM (Science, Technology, Engineering and Math) concepts. Children interact with real materials, fostering imagination and attention to detail without any screens.

b). **Educational Board Games:** Classic board games adapted for younger audiences like Scrabble Junior and Math Bingo can introduce vocabulary and math in an interactive, social way. It helps to improve the vocabulary, math, social skills and strategic thinking and encourage family participation, which makes learning a shared experience and reduces the urge to reach for digital devices.

c). **Puzzle Games:** Physical puzzles and tangram sets involve arranging pieces to fit specific patterns or shapes. These games are excellent for hand-eye coordination and spatial awareness. Spatial reasoning, logic, patience and fine motor skills. Tangible puzzles can captivate kids without needing a screen, helping to build focus and perseverance.

d). **Science Experiment Kits:** These kits provide materials and instructions for at-home science experiments, covering topics like geology, chemistry and biology. Scientific thinking, observation, patience and experimentation. Kids work with real objects and observe reactions, which fosters a love for science without screens.

e). **Outdoor Exploration Games:** Organize outdoor scavenger hunts or nature bingo, where kids must find specific items in nature or complete challenges related to the environment. Observation, curiosity, physical activity and critical thinking. These activities engage children with the outdoors, encouraging exercise and an appreciation for nature instead of screen time.

f). **Educational Card Games:** Educational card games like Uno, Brain Quest or subject-specific flashcards can turn learning into quick, interactive sessions with friends or family. Memory, logic, math, quick thinking and social skills. Compact and easy to play anywhere, these games provide screen-free fun, especially effective for group play.

g). **Think Fun Games:** Think Fun offers educational board games that require logical thinking to solve puzzles, often alone or cooperatively. Logic, problem-solving, spatial awareness and planning. These games are tactile and don't require a screen, fostering focus and critical thinking without digital devices.

h). **Story Cubes:** Story Cubes are dice with different images on each side, encouraging children to create a story based on the rolled images. Creativity, vocabulary, imagination and storytelling. This game is an imaginative activity that requires no screens, keeping children engaged through creativity and communication.

i). **Crafting Kits:** Craft kits, such as those for making jewellery, painting or creating model animals, allow kids to build something unique with step-by-step guidance. Creativity, focus, patience and fine motor skills. These hands-on activities let kids immerse themselves in a project, encouraging mindfulness and creativity without screens.

j). **Educational Building Sets:** Magna-Tiles and K'NEX sets encourage kids to construct 3D shapes and structures, developing spatial reasoning and engineering concepts. Engineering basics, creativity, motor skills and spatial awareness. Children physically build structures, engaging their hands and minds in constructive play, ideal for screen-free learning.

Each of these games is designed to make learning engaging, while keeping children away from Mobile/ TV screens, encouraging meaningful interactions with physical materials, creativity and cooperative play. Introducing these types of games helps establish a balanced approach to play and learning that minimizes mobile dependence.

॥ ॐ ॥

10

Reward System

Implement a positive reinforcement system for adhering to screen time limit. Offer rewards like extra playtime, a special outing or a small treat, when children demonstrate responsible device usage.

Implementing a reward system can be an effective way to motivate individuals, especially students, to reduce mobile device addiction and cultivate healthier screen habits. Here's how you can set up a reward system:

a). **Define Clear Goals**: Clearly outline the specific goals or behaviors you want to encourage. For instance, reducing daily screen time, adhering to designated screen-free times or engaging in alternative activities.

b). **Choose Rewards**: Determine a list of rewards that would be appealing to the individual. These rewards can range from small treats to meaningful experiences.

c). **Assign Point System**: Create a point system where individuals earn points for meeting the defined goals or behaviors. For instance, they could earn points for each hour of reduced screen time.

d). **Track Progress**: Keep track of the points earned by individuals. You can use a physical chart, a digital app or a simple notebook.

e). **Set Milestones**: Establish milestones at certain point thresholds. When individuals reach a milestone, they can earn a predetermined reward.

f). **Regularly Review and Reward**: Periodically review the progress with the individual. Celebrate their achievements and offer the rewards they have earned.

g). **Encourage Consistency**: Emphasize the importance of consistent effort in earning points and achieving goals.

h). **Offer Varied Rewards**: Mix up the rewards to keep the motivation high. Offer a combination of small, immediate rewards and larger, more impactful rewards.

i). **Tailor Rewards to Interests**: Customize rewards based on the individual's interests. If they enjoy art, a reward could be a set of art supplies. If they love outdoor activities, a reward could be a nature outing.

j). **Involve Them in Reward Selection**: Allow individuals to participate in selecting rewards. This gives them a sense of ownership and motivation to work towards their chosen rewards.

k). **Make It a Family or Group Effort**: Extend the reward system to involve the entire family or a group of friends. This can foster healthy competition and camaraderie.

l). **Celebrate Achievements**: Celebrate not only the milestones but also the effort put into reaching them. Acknowledge the commitment to positive change.

m). **Gradually Adjust Goals**: As individuals make progress, gradually adjust the goals to continue challenging them while ensuring they are attainable.

n). **Keep the System Positive**: Focus on positive reinforcement rather than punishment. Encourage and support their efforts, rather than criticizing failures.

o).   **Reflect and Adjust**: Regularly assess the effectiveness of the reward system. Adjust the goals and rewards as needed based on the individual's response and progress.

Remember that the reward system should be designed to support positive behavior change and create a sense of accomplishment. The rewards themselves don't need to be extravagant; they should serve as a tangible acknowledgment of their efforts toward reducing mobile addiction and embracing healthier habits.

|| ॐ ||

11

Digital Detox Days

Designate specific days each week or month as "digital detox" days. During these times, the family or classroom avoids screens altogether and focuses on in-person interactions and other activities.

Absolutely, implementing digital detox days can be a highly effective strategy to reduce mobile addiction in children, students and adults as well. Here's how you can go about it:

a). **Plan Ahead:** Decide on the frequency of digital detox days, whether it's once a week, once a month or at another interval. Make sure all family members or students are aware of the upcoming detox days well in advance.

b). **Set Clear Expectations:** Explain the purpose of digital detox days to everyone involved. Let them know that it's an opportunity to disconnect from screens, engage in face-to-face interactions and explore different activities.

c). **Activities Planning:** Prepare a list of alternative activities that can be done during the detox days. This might include outdoor games, puzzles, board games, art and craft projects, reading or cooking together. Having a variety of options can keep everyone engaged.

d). **Device Collection:** On the morning of the detox day, collect all mobile devices, tablets and other screens from family members or students. Store them in a designated place to avoid temptation.

e). **Lead by Example:** Adults should actively participate in digital detox days and demonstrate enthusiasm for the activities planned. Children and students are more likely to follow suit, when they see adults fully engaged.

f). **Engage in Group Activities:** Organize activities that involve the entire family or classroom. This fosters bonding and interaction without the distraction of screens.

g). **Explore Nature:** If possible, spend time outdoors during the digital detox days. Nature walks, picnics or gardening can provide a refreshing break from technology.

h). **Encourage Creativity:** Offer opportunities for creative expression, such as drawing, painting, writing or building. This can stimulate imagination and help children and students discover new interests.

i). **Reflect and Discuss:** At the end of the detox day, gather everyone together to share their experiences. Discuss what they enjoyed, what challenges they faced and any insights gained.

j). **Celebrate Achievements:** Acknowledge the efforts of everyone who participated in the digital detox day. Consider offering simple rewards or incentives to reinforce the positive experience.

k). **Gradual Progress:** If digital detox days are new for your family or classroom, start gradually. Begin with shorter periods and gradually extend the duration as everyone becomes more comfortable with the idea.

l). **Open Dialogue:** Use the experience as a conversation starter about the importance of balance in technology use. Discuss the benefits of spending quality time away from screens.

By consistently practicing digital detox days, you can help children and students develop a healthier relationship with technology, recognize the value of in-person interactions and create a stronger sense of connection with in the family or classroom.

॥ ॐ ॥

12

Teach Time Management

Help children develop effective time management skills by teaching them how to prioritize tasks, set goals and allocate time for different activities.

Absolutely, teaching time management skills is a valuable approach to reducing mobile addiction and promoting a balanced lifestyle for children and students. Here's how you can help them develop effective time management skills:

a). **Explain the Importance:** Start by discussing with children and students why time management is essential. Help them understand that good time management can lead to better productivity, reduced stress and more time for enjoyable activities.

b). **Set Clear Goals:** Teach them how to set both short-term and long-term goals. Break down larger goals into smaller, achievable tasks. This can give them a sense of direction and purpose.

c). **Use a Planner or Calendar:** Introduce them to the concept of using planners, calendars or digital tools to organize tasks and activities. Help them schedule study time, extracurricular activities and leisure activities.

d). **Prioritize Tasks:** Teach them how to identify tasks that are urgent and important versus those that can wait. This helps them allocate time wisely and avoid procrastination.

e). **Create a To-Do List:** Encourage them to create a daily or weekly to-do list. Crossing off completed tasks can be motivating and provide a sense of accomplishment. Guide them in allocating specific time blocks for different tasks. For example – set aside dedicated time for studying, hobbies, socializing and screen time.

f). **Practice Time Tracking:** Have them track how they spend their time for a few days. This can help them become aware of how much time they're devoting to various activities, including mobile device usage.

g). **Limit Multitasking:** Explain the drawbacks of multitasking and encourage them to focus on one task at a time. This can lead to better concentration and efficiency.

h). **Set Time Limits for Screens:** Help them set reasonable limits for screen time. Collaboratively establish rules for device usage during study hours, mealtimes and before bedtime.

i). **Use Breaks Wisely:** Teach them the importance of taking breaks during study or work sessions. Short breaks can help recharge their focus and energy.

j). **Reflect and Adjust:** Regularly reflect on their time management practices. Encourage them to assess what's working well and make adjustments as needed.

k). **Encourage Self-Discipline:** Emphasize the importance of sticking to the schedule they create. Building self-discipline gradually reduces the likelihood of excessive mobile device use.

l). **Be a Supportive Guide:** Offer guidance and support as they develop their time management skills. Be patient and help them learn from their mistakes.

By equipping children and students with strong time management skills, you empower them to make conscious choices about how they spend their time, which can significantly contribute to reducing mobile addiction and promoting a healthier lifestyle.

॥ ॐ ॥

13

Seek Professional Help

Professional help provides a structured way to assess the extent of mobile addiction. Mental health professionals can help individuals recognize the signs of addiction or identifying the actual problem, such as excessive use, neglecting responsibilities or feelings of anxiety etc. when separated from their devices. This identification is a crucial first step in addressing the issue.

a). **Personalized Treatment Plans**: Therapists can develop tailored treatment plans based on individual needs and circumstances. These plans might include behavioural therapies, cognitive strategies and goal-setting techniques aimed at reducing mobile device dependency and promoting healthier habits. Personalization increases the effectiveness of the treatment.

b). **Cognitive Behavioural Therapy (CBT)**: CBT is a common therapeutic approach used to treat mobile addiction. It focuses on identifying negative thought patterns and behaviours related to device use. By reframing these thoughts and developing coping strategies, individuals can learn to manage their mobile usage more effectively.

c). **Family Therapy**: Involving family members in the therapeutic process can enhance support systems and create a collective approach to managing mobile use. Family therapy can address communication issues, establish boundaries around technology and foster a supportive environment for recovery.

d). **Support Groups**: Support groups provide a platform for individuals to share their experiences and struggles with mobile addiction. Connecting with others facing similar challenges can foster a sense of community, reduce feelings of isolation and motivate individuals to make positive changes.

e). **Mindfulness and Relaxation Techniques**: Professionals often introduce mindfulness and relaxation strategies as part of the treatment plan. Techniques such as meditation, deep breathing and yoga can help individuals manage stress and anxiety, making it easier to resist the urge to use mobile devices excessively.

f). **Behavioural Assessments**: Therapists can conduct behavioural assessments to help individuals understand their mobile usage patterns. This includes evaluating how much time is spent on devices, the types of activities engaged in and the emotional responses associated with mobile use. Such assessments can reveal insights that inform change.

g). **Skill Building**: Professional guidance can help individuals develop essential skills for managing mobile usage, such as setting limits, creating schedules and finding alternative activities. These skills empower individuals to regain control over their time and reduce reliance on mobile devices for entertainment or social interaction.

h). **Education on Risks**: Mental health professionals can provide education about the risks associated with excessive mobile use, including its impact on mental health, sleep, relationships and productivity. This knowledge can serve as a motivating factor for individuals to seek help and make positive changes.

i). **Co-Occurring Issues**: Many individuals struggling with mobile addiction may also face underlying mental health issues, such as depression, anxiety or stress. Seeking professional help ensures that these co-occurring disorders are addressed, leading to a more holistic approach to treatment and improved overall well-being.

j). **On-going Support and Follow-Up**: Continuous support through follow-up sessions is critical for long-term success. Professionals can help individuals monitor their progress, celebrate successes and make necessary adjustments to their treatment plans. This on-going relationship fosters accountability and encourages sustained efforts to reduce mobile addiction.

k). **Crisis Intervention**: In cases where mobile addiction leads to severe consequences, such as social withdrawal or academic failure, professionals can provide crisis intervention strategies. These interventions ensure that individuals receive immediate support and resources to help them regain control of their lives.

By emphasizing the importance of seeking professional help, we can create pathways for individuals struggling with mobile addiction to find the support they need. This proactive approach can lead to healthier relationships with technology, improved mental health and a balanced lifestyle.

|| ॐ ||

14

Join Support Groups

Understanding the importance of community, support groups create a sense of community among individuals facing similar challenges, such as mobile addiction. This shared experience fosters an environment, where members can openly discuss their struggles, fears and successes without fear of judgment. Feeling understood and supported is a crucial aspect of recovery.

a). **Sharing Experiences and Strategies**: Members of support groups can share personal stories and coping strategies that have helped them manage their mobile usage. This exchange of ideas can provide new perspectives and practical solutions that individuals may not have considered on their own. Learning from others' experiences can be both enlightening and motivating.

b). **Accountability**: Being part of a support group encourages accountability. Members can set goals for reducing mobile use and share their progress with the group. This accountability can reinforce commitment and provide the encouragement needed to stay on track, making it harder to slip back into old habits.

c). **Emotional Support**: Support groups offer emotional support that can be invaluable for individuals struggling with mobile addiction. Members can express their feelings, fears and frustrations in a safe space, helping to alleviate feelings of isolation and anxiety. This emotional validation can be a critical component of the healing process.

d). **Access to Resources**: Many support groups provide access to additional resources, such as literature on mobile addiction, workshops and educational materials. These resources can enhance understanding of the issues at hand and offer guidance on effective strategies for managing mobile use.

e). **Facilitated Discussions**: Many support groups are led by trained facilitators who can guide discussions and provide insights into overcoming mobile addiction. These facilitators often have experience in addiction counselling and can help steer conversations toward productive outcomes.

f). **Developing New Coping Mechanisms**: Support groups can introduce alternative activities and coping mechanisms to replace excessive mobile use. Members can share hobbies, interests and activities that have helped them reduce their screen time, fostering a culture of exploration and personal growth.

g). **Encouragement for Professional Help**: Being part of a support group can encourage individuals to seek professional help if needed. Hearing about others' experiences with therapy or counselling can motivate members to consider these options for a more comprehensive approach to recovery.

h). **Building Lasting Friendships**: Many individuals find lasting friendships within support groups. These connections can extend beyond the group setting, providing on-going support and encouragement outside of meetings. Having friends who understand the journey can make recovery more enjoyable and fulfilling.

i). **Diverse Perspectives**: Support groups often comprise individuals from various backgrounds, ages and experiences. This diversity allows members to gain different perspectives on mobile addiction and recovery, enriching their understanding and approach to managing their own habits.

j). **Safe Space for Vulnerability**: A support group provides a safe space, where individuals can be vulnerable without fear of judgment. This environment encourages open and honest communication, which is essential for personal growth and healing.

k). **Regular Meetings and Consistency**: Regular meetings help maintain momentum in the recovery process. Consistency reinforces commitment to change and allows for continuous support and encouragement from peers.

By promoting the idea of joining support groups, we can facilitate community connections that empower individuals to address their mobile addiction collaboratively. This supportive network can lead to significant positive changes in their relationship with technology, enhancing their overall well-being.

|| ॐ ||

15

Workshops and Seminars

Workshops and seminars are powerful tools in the fight against 'Mobile Addiction', bringing people together to understand, discuss and tackle the issues surrounding excessive screen time. Through hands-on activities, expert guidance and real-life examples, these sessions offer participants effective strategies for managing mobile use. Tailored for all ages, workshops and seminars encourage collective learning, support and empowerment. They not only raise awareness but also provide actionable steps for lasting change, helping individuals and communities develop healthier relationships with technology. These gatherings spark meaningful conversations, inspire personal growth and ultimately strengthen our commitment to a balanced, digitally mindful life.

a). **Educational Workshops on Mobile Addiction:**

Objective: Conduct workshops that educate participants about the impact of mobile addiction on mental health, social skills and overall well-being. These sessions can cover statistics, personal stories and expert insights to raise awareness about the issues surrounding excessive mobile usage.

Format: Invite psychologists, educators or health professionals to lead these workshops, incorporating interactive elements such as discussions, Q&A sessions and group activities. Participants can engage in exercises that reflect on their mobile use habits.

b).   Skill-Building Seminars:

Objective: Organize seminars focused on building skills that promote healthier screen habits. Topics could include effective time management, stress reduction techniques and mindfulness practices that encourage individuals to find balance in their lives.

Format: Utilize a mix of presentations, hands-on activities and group discussions to engage participants. Encourage to share their experiences and strategies for managing their mobile device use.

c).   Creative Workshops:

Objective: Host creative workshops that offer alternatives to mobile device usage. Activities could include art, music, dance or writing, allowing participants to express themselves in ways that promote emotional well-being and creativity.

Format: Collaborate with local artists, musicians or writers to lead these sessions. Participants can create projects that they can share, fostering a sense of community and encouraging on-going engagement in creative pursuits.

d).   Parent-Child Workshops:

Objective: Organize workshops specifically designed for parents and their children to learn about healthy technology use together. These sessions can facilitate open discussions about mobile device usage and its effects on family dynamics.

Format: Include activities that promote teamwork and communication, such as role-playing or collaborative problem-solving tasks. Encourage families to develop collective agreement on screen time and alternative activities.

e).   Mindfulness and Wellness Workshops:

Objective: Focus on workshops that teach mindfulness and wellness techniques to help individuals manage stress and anxiety without resorting to mobile devices. Practices such as meditation, yoga and deep breathing exercises can be introduced.

Format: Hire certified instructors to guide participants through mindfulness practices. Include sessions on developing personal wellness plans that prioritize self-care and reduce dependence on screens.

f). Digital Detox Challenges:

Objective: Launch workshops that promote digital detox challenges, encouraging participants to reduce their screen time for a specific period. These challenges can create a supportive environment for individuals to share their experiences and strategies for coping without their devices.

Format: Create a structured program that includes weekly check-ins, group discussions and activities that participants can do instead of using their devices. Provide resources and tools to help them succeed in the challenge.

g). Workshops on Technology Management:

Objective: Teach participants about technology management, including how to set boundaries for mobile device usage, utilize parental controls and find applications that promote productivity and focus.

Format: Provide demonstrations on how to use various apps and tools to manage screen time effectively. Encourage participants to share their favourite productivity tools and techniques.

h). Guest Speaker Series:

Objective: Organize a series of talks featuring experts in mental health, technology and education who can share their insights on mobile addiction and its impact on society.

Format: Schedule monthly or quarterly guest speakers to present on various topics related to mobile usage. Encourage audience interaction through Q&A sessions, allowing participant to engage directly with the experts.

i). **Collaboration with Schools and Community Centres**:

Objective: Partner with local schools and community centres to host workshops and seminars, making these learning opportunities accessible to a broader audience.

Format: Work with educators and community leaders to identify relevant topics and tailor workshops to meet the needs of different age groups. Provide resources for parents to support their children in managing mobile device use.

j). **Feedback and Follow-Up**:

Objective: After each workshop or seminar, gather feedback from participants to assess the effectiveness of the sessions and identify areas for improvement. This input can help tailor future workshops to better meet the needs of the audience.

Format: Use surveys or group discussions to collect feedback. Additionally, consider providing follow-up resources or support groups for participants to continue their learning and engagement.

By implementing workshops and seminars focused on mobile addiction, individuals can gain valuable knowledge and skills to help them navigate their technology use more effectively. These interactive experiences can foster community support and empower participants to make positive changes in their lives.

|| ॐ ||

16

Parental Guidance

Parental guidance is essential in helping children navigate the challenges of 'Mobile Addiction' in a world increasingly defined by digital interaction. Parents play a pivotal role in setting healthy boundaries, modeling mind-ful tech habits and encouraging balanced lifestyles that emphasize offline activities and personal connections. This chapter explores practical ways for parents to actively support their children's well-being by promoting responsible mobile use. Through strategies, resources and open communication, parents can become effective role models and advocates for positive digital habits, ultimately empowering their children to thrive in a balanced, tech-savvy future.

a). **Establishing Open Communication:**

Objective: Foster an environment where children feel comfortable discussing their technology use, including any fears or pressures they may experience.

Approach: Encourage parents to ask open-ended questions about their children's experiences with mobile devices, including social media interactions and online gaming. This helps children articulate their feelings and fears.

b). **Setting Clear Boundaries:**

Objective: Help parents establish clear and reasonable boundaries regarding mobile device usage. These boundaries should be communicated and agreed upon by both parents and children.

Approach: Guide parents in creating a family technology agreement that outlines when and where devices can be used. Include rules for screen time limits, device-free zones and specific times for family interaction.

c). **Educating about Online Risks**:

Objective: Equip parents with knowledge about the potential risks associated with excessive mobile usage, including cyber bullying, online predators and exposure to inappropriate content.

Approach: Organize informational sessions or distribute resources that explain the dangers of mobile technology. Encourage parents to discuss these risks openly with their children helping them understand how to stay safe online.

d). **Promoting Healthy Alternatives**:

Objective: Encourage parents to guide their children towards alternative activities that promote a balanced lifestyle and reduce reliance on mobile devices.

Approach: Suggest engaging family activities such as outdoor sports, board games or creative hobbies. Highlight the importance of nurturing interests outside of technology to cultivate well-rounded development.

e). **Addressing Fears of Isolation**:

Objective: Help parents manage their children's fears of being left out or isolated due to reduced screen time. Children may worry about missing out on social interactions or trends.

Approach: Discuss the importance of real-life connections and encourage parents to facilitate social interactions that do not involve screens. Plan a regular play dates or group activities that emphasize face-to-face communication.

f). **Modelling Healthy Technology Use:**

Objective: Encourage parents to demonstrate healthy technology habits in their own lives, reinforcing the behaviours they want to see in their children.

Approach: Suggest parents engage in device-free family meals, outings and activities. This sets a positive example and shows children that it's possible to enjoy life without constantly being on their phones.

g). **Encouraging Emotional Intelligence:**

Objective: Help parents teach their children to recognize and manage their emotions related to mobile device usage, including anxiety, fear or loneliness.

Approach: Introduce parents to emotional regulation techniques that they can share with their children, such as deep breathing, mindfulness practices or journaling about their feelings related to screen time.

h). **Monitoring and Adjusting:**

Objective: Guide parents in regularly monitoring their children's mobile usage and adjusting boundaries as necessary based on observed behaviour and changing circumstances.

Approach: Suggest using apps that track screen time or having regular family discussions about technology use. Encourage parents to be flexible and willing to adapt rules as children grow and develop.

i). **Involving Professionals When Necessary:**

Objective: Help parents recognize when professional intervention may be needed. If a child's mobile addiction is significantly impacting their daily life, seeking help from a counsellor or psychologist may be necessary.

Approach: Provide resources for finding qualified professionals who specialize in technology addiction or child psychology. Encourage parents to act proactively to ensure the child's well-being.

j). **Creating a Support Network**:

Objective: Encourage parents to connect with other parents facing similar challenges, fostering a support network for sharing experiences and strategies.

Approach: Suggest organizing or joining parent groups or forums focused on technology use. This provides a space for discussing concerns, sharing successes and gaining insights from others' experiences.

k). **Empowering Children through Education**:

Objective: Teach children about the potential consequences of mobile addiction and empower them to make informed choices regarding their technology use.

Approach: Collaborate with schools to include technology literacy programs in the curriculum. This education can help children understand the importance of balancing screen time with other aspects of life.

By focusing on parental guidance and fear management, families can work together to create a supportive environment that encourages healthy technology use. Parents play a crucial role in helping their children navigate the challenges of mobile addiction while fostering resilience and emotional intelligence.

|| ॐ ||

17

Scheduled Usage

Scheduled use is a structured approach to managing mobile screen time, designed to encourage purposeful and balanced engagement with technology. By creating set times for mobile activities, this method helps individuals prioritize their daily routines and reduce unnecessary screen time. This chapter explores effective strategies for scheduling mobile use to instill a sense of discipline, improve focus and minimize distractions. With a well-planned approach, scheduled use enables both children and adults to enjoy the benefits of technology without letting it interfere with personal growth, relationships or productivity. Ultimately, it fosters a healthier, more intentional digital lifestyle.

a). **Establish Clear Usage Guidelines**: Set specific rules around when and how mobile devices can be used. Create a family agreement outlining acceptable screen time limits for different activities, such as social media, gaming or video streaming. Make sure everyone understands and agrees to these guidelines to foster accountability.

b). **Designate Device-Free Zones**: Encourage mind-full usage of mobile devices by creating areas in the home where devices are not allowed. Identify certain spaces, such as the dining room or bedrooms, as device-free zones. This promotes healthier interactions and helps establish boundaries between device usage and family time.

c). **Set Specific Time Blocks for Usage**: Help individuals learn to manage their time effectively while using mobile devices. Schedule specific time blocks for device usage throughout the day. For example, allow 30 minutes for social media after homework is completed or designate an hour for gaming on weekends. This structure encourages a balanced approach to screen time.

d). **Use Technology to Manage Time**: Leverage apps and features to help monitor and limit screen time. Utilize built-in features on devices or third-party apps that allow users to set time limits on specific applications or overall device usage. Review usage statistics regularly to ensure adherence to the established schedule.

e). **Encourage Planning for Screen Time**: Promote intentional use of mobile devices rather than mindless scrolling or gaming. Before accessing devices, encourage individuals to plan what they intend to do online, such as watching a specific show, reading an article or participating in a video call. This reduces aimless use and increases productivity.

f). **Balance Digital and Non-Digital Activities**: Ensure that mobile usage is balanced with other important activities in life. When scheduling usage, encourage individuals to allocate time for non-digital activities as well, such as reading, exercising or spending time with family. This promotes a well-rounded lifestyle and reduces reliance on screens for entertainment.

g). **Create a Weekly Schedule**: Develop a routine that incorporates both mobile usage and other activities. Help individuals create a weekly schedule that includes designated times for mobile device usage, homework, hobbies, family time and outdoor activities. Visualizing their week can help reinforce the importance of balance.

h). **Implement Time Limits for Each Session**: Prevent extended, uninterrupted periods of mobile device use. Set a timer for each mobile device session, allowing 30 to 60 minutes for use, followed by a break. This practice encourages breaks and helps maintain focus on other tasks and responsibilities.

i). **Encourage Regular Breaks**: Reduce fatigue and promote healthy device habits by incorporating breaks. Encourage individuals to take breaks during extended device usage to stretch, hydrate or engage in a quick physical activity. This not only refreshes the mind but also combats the physical effects of prolonged screen time.

j). **Review and Adjust the Schedule Regularly**: Ensure the usage schedule remains effective and adaptable to changing needs. Periodically review the established schedule with family members. Discuss what is working well and what might need to be adjusted. This collaborative approach fosters communication and ownership of the device usage plan.

k). **Set Consequences for Breaking Guidelines**: Foster accountability and adherence to the scheduled usage plan. Agree on consequences for breaking the established screen time rules, such as temporary loss of device privileges. Ensure these consequences are fair and consistently enforced.

l). **Lead by Example**: Encourage healthy mobile usage habits by modelling appropriate behaviour. Parents and guardians should adhere to their own scheduled usage to demonstrate commitment to the plan. Showing a balanced approach to technology will positively influence children's attitudes toward mobile devices.

m). **Communicate Openly About Usage**: Foster a culture of transparency regarding mobile device use. Encourage open discussions about how mobile devices affect daily life and relationships. Share experiences and feelings about screen time, promoting mutual understanding and support within the family.

n). **Incorporate Family Time into the Schedule**: Strengthen family bonds by ensuring time spent together is prioritized. Schedule regular family activities that do not involve screens, such as game nights, outdoor adventures or movie nights. This fosters quality time and reinforces the importance of family connections.

o). **Encourage Participation in Offline Activities**: Provide engaging alternatives to screen time that promote creativity and social interaction. Suggest activities such as art and craft projects, cooking or community service as scheduled alternatives to mobile device use. This encourages a diverse range of interests beyond technology.

By implementing **scheduled usage** of mobile devices, individuals can cultivate a healthier relationship with technology, ensuring that it enhances rather than dominates their lives. This structured approach promotes balance, accountability and meaningful engagement in various activities, helping to combat mobile addiction effectively.

॥ ॐ ॥

18

Mindfulness and Meditation

Mindfulness and meditation offer powerful techniques to counteract the effects of 'Mobile Addiction' by fostering greater self-awareness and emotional control. These practices help individuals reconnect with the present moment, reducing the urge to mindlessly check screens and creating space for intentional, fulfilling activities. This chapter introduces simple yet effective mindfulness exercises and meditation techniques tailored to ease the mental strain of digital overload. By incorporating mindfulness and meditation into daily routines, both children/ students and adults can cultivate a healthier relationship with technology, gaining clarity, focus and a renewed appreciation for life beyond the screen.

a). **Understanding Mindfulness:**

Objective: Help individuals grasp the concept of mindfulness as being present and fully engaged in the moment without distraction.

Approach: Discuss the benefits of mindfulness, including reduced stress, improved focus and enhanced emotional regulation. Emphasize how being mindful can counteract the compulsive nature of mobile device use.

b). **Introduce Meditation Practices:**

Objective: Encourage regular meditation as a tool for cultivating mindfulness.

Approach: Start with simple breathing exercises, such as focusing on the breath for a few minutes daily. Gradually introduce guided meditations that can be accessed via apps or online platforms, making it easier for beginners to engage.

c). **Create a Dedicated Mindfulness Space**:

Objective: Establish a conducive environment for mindfulness and meditation practices.

Approach: Set up a quiet space at home where individuals can practice mindfulness and meditation without interruptions. Encourage them to personalize this space with calming elements, such as cushions, candles or plants.

d). **Encourage Mindful Breathing**:

Objective: Teach the importance of breath awareness in managing stress and reducing mobile device reliance.

Approach: Introduce exercises that focus on deep, slow breathing. Encourage individuals to pause throughout the day and take a few deep breaths, especially before reaching for their devices.

e). **Incorporate Mindfulness into Daily Activities**:

Objective: Help individuals practice mindfulness beyond formal meditation sessions.

Approach: Encourage mindfulness during everyday tasks, such as eating, walking or even washing dishes. Prompt individuals to focus on their sensations and experiences during these activities, which can help reduce mindless mobile usage.

f). **Practice Digital Mindfulness**:

Objective: Cultivate awareness of how mobile devices impact mental and emotional well-being.

Approach: Teach individuals to recognize their triggers for mobile device use and encourage them to pause before picking up their phones. Ask them to reflect on their feelings and motivations for wanting to check their devices.

g). **Mindfulness Apps and Resources**:

Objective: Provide tools and resources to support mindfulness and meditation practices.

Approach: Introduce apps and online resources that offer guided meditations, mindfulness exercises and tracking tools. Some popular options include Headspace, Calm and Insight Timer, which can be useful for beginners.

h). **Set Mindfulness Reminders**:

Objective: Encourage consistent mindfulness practices throughout the day.

Approach: Use reminders or notifications on devices to prompt short mindfulness breaks, such as taking a few deep breaths, practicing gratitude or engaging in a quick meditation session.

i). **Encourage Group Meditation Sessions**:

Objective: Foster a sense of community and support in mindfulness practices.

Approach: Suggest participating in group meditation classes or online sessions, which can motivate individuals to stick to their practice and provide accountability.

j). **Teach Body Scan Techniques**:

Objective: Enhance awareness of bodily sensations and promote relaxation.

Approach: Introduce body scan meditation, where individuals focus on different parts of their body to release tension and cultivate relaxation. This practice can help individuals become more attuned to their physical state and reduce the urge to reach for devices.

k). Promote Journaling for Reflection:

Objective: Encourage self-reflection and awareness of mobile usage patterns.

Approach: Suggest keeping a mindfulness journal to document thoughts and feelings after meditation sessions. Encourage individuals to reflect on how their device usage aligns with their mindfulness goals and to set intentions for improvement.

l). Incorporate Gratitude Practices:

Objective: Shift focus from devices to positive aspects of life.

Approach: Encourage individuals to express gratitude daily by noting down things they appreciate, which can reduce negative feelings often associated with mobile device use and promote a positive mindset.

m). Connect Mindfulness with Technology Use:

Objective: Help individuals recognize the impact of technology on their well-being.

Approach: Discuss how mindfulness can enhance their relationship with technology, helping them become more selective about their usage and reducing unnecessary scrolling or gaming.

n). Establish a Mindfulness Routine:

Objective: Create a consistent practice for individuals to follow.

Approach: Help individuals establish a daily mindfulness routine that incorporates meditation, mindful breathing and moments of reflection. Consistency can lead to lasting changes in their relationship with technology.

o). **Encourage Mindful Screen Time:**

Objective: Transform how individuals engage with their devices.

Approach: Teach individuals to approach screen time mindfully by selecting specific, purposeful activities, such as reading educational content or engaging with creative applications, rather than mindlessly browsing social media.

p). **Utilize Mindfulness Techniques for Stress Management:**

Objective: Equip individuals with tools to handle stress without resorting to device use.

Approach: Introduce mindfulness techniques, such as visualization or progressive muscle relaxation, to manage stress. This can help individuals find healthier coping mechanisms when they feel overwhelmed.

q). **Foster Emotional Regulation:**

Objective: Help individuals understand and manage their emotions related to device use.

Approach: Teach emotional regulation skills through mindfulness, helping individuals identify feelings that trigger mobile device use and develop alternative strategies for coping.

r). **Promote Mindful Social Interactions:**

Objective: Enhance face-to-face communication and relationships.

Approach: Encourage individuals to practice mindfulness during social interactions by actively listening and being present, rather than being distracted by their devices. This can lead to deeper connections and reduce the urge to rely on screens for socializing.

By integrating **mindfulness and meditation** practices into daily life, individuals can cultivate a greater awareness of their device usage patterns and learn to approach technology with intention and balance. These practices can significantly contribute to reducing mobile addiction, enhancing well-being and promoting healthier lifestyle choices.

॥ ॐ ॥

19

Interactive Storytelling

Interactive storytelling offers an engaging and creative way to address 'Mobile Addiction', especially for younger audiences. By combining storytelling with hands-on activities, this approach makes learning about screen time management more enjoyable and impactful. Through interactive stories, children/ students can explore scenarios, make decisions and experience the consequences of healthy or excessive mobile use. This chapter highlights the benefits of using storytelling as a tool for teaching digital mindfulness, empowering kids to understand and practice balanced tech habits in a fun, memorable way. With interactive storytelling, managing screen time becomes a shared adventure, sparking meaningful discussion and lessons that extend beyond the story itself.

a). **Engagement through Participation/Interactive Nature**: Unlike passive screen time, interactive storytelling invites participants to actively engage with the narrative. This could involve making choices that affect the story's outcome, fostering a sense of agency and involvement.

b). **Digital Storytelling Tools/Leveraging Technology**: Introduce children and adults to user-friendly storytelling platforms that encourage creativity. Should allow users to craft their narratives, merging technology with imaginative expression rather than passive consumption.

c). **The Art of Oral Storytelling/ Connecting Through Voices**: Encourage storytelling sessions where children narrate their favorite tales or create new ones. This oral tradition not only enhances communication skills but also builds confidence in expressing ideas without the need for screens.

d). **Collaborative Story Creation/ Team Effort**: Organize group storytelling activities where participants contribute to a shared story. This can be done in classrooms, at home or in community centers, promoting teamwork and reducing isolation often associated with mobile device use.

e). **Incorporating Visual Elements/ Bringing Stories to Life**: Use props, illustrations or puppets to enhance storytelling experiences. These tactile elements make stories more vivid and engaging, helping to draw participants away from their screens and into a world of imagination.

f). **Story-Based Learning Approaches/ Educational Narratives**: Integrate stories into educational settings by developing lessons around compelling narratives. This approach helps students connect emotionally with the subject matter, making learning enjoyable and interactive, without the distractions of mobile devices.

g). **Empowering through Story Writing/ Fostering Creativity**: Encourage children to write their own stories, fostering creativity and self-expression. Provide resources like journals or digital tools to help them illustrate their ideas, promoting a sense of accomplishment and reducing screen time.

h). **Workshops for Skill Development/ Structured Learning**: Host workshops focused on various storytelling techniques. These sessions can cover everything from character development to improvisation, providing participants with tools to express themselves creatively without relying on mobile device.

i). **Exploring Interactive Books/ Choice-Driven Reading**: Provide access to interactive books where readers make decisions that steer the story. This engaging format helps develop critical thinking skills and keeps readers invested in the story without resorting to screens.

j). **Mindful Technology Use/ Balancing Digital Engagement**: While technology can facilitate storytelling, it's essential to use it mindfully. Encourage the use of storytelling podcasts or audiobooks, which allow for immersive experiences without the need for constant screen interaction.

k). **Reflective Storytelling Practices/ Introspection through Narratives**: Encourage participants to share personal stories that reflect their experiences. This practice can enhance self-awareness and empathy, serving as a powerful alternative to excessive mobile device use.

l). **Establishing Storytelling Clubs/ Community Connections**: Create clubs dedicated to storytelling where members gather to share and develop their narratives. This communal aspect provides social interaction and encourages engagement in a constructive manner.

m). **Cultural Exploration Through Stories/ Diverse Perspectives**: Encourage storytelling that draws from different cultural traditions. This exploration can foster a deeper understanding of the world and reduce the desire to escape into mobile screens.

n). **Using Storytelling for Problem-Solving/ Creative Solutions**: Guide participants to create stories that tackle real-life challenges, helping them brainstorm and reflect on solutions. This approach promotes critical thinking and can effectively redirect focus from devices.

o). **Music and Movement Integration/ Dynamic Storytelling:** Combine storytelling with music and physical activity. This approach makes narratives more engaging and encourages participants to express themselves through movement, which can be a refreshing break from screens.

p). **Intergenerational Story Sharing/ Bridging Generations:** Organize storytelling sessions that connect children with older adults. This exchange enriches relationships and provides valuable lessons without the need for digital distractions.

q). **Engaging Story Challenges/ Fun and Creativity:** Set up friendly competitions where participants create stories based on specific prompts within a time limit. This not only sparks creativity but also offers a lively alternative to mobile device use.

r). **Environmental Awareness Through Narratives/ Eco-Conscious Storytelling:** Encourage stories that address environmental themes, promoting awareness and responsibility for the planet. This focus can inspire interest in nature and reduce reliance on digital entertainment.

s). **Interactive Story Games/ Game-Enhanced Narratives:** Develop games that incorporate storytelling elements, such as role-playing games where participants shape the narrative. This combines the enjoyment of gaming with interactive storytelling, promoting engagements without screens.

t). **Celebrating Storytelling Festivals/ Community Events:** Host festivals dedicated to the art of storytelling, providing a platform for individuals to showcase their talents. Such events foster community spirit and emphasize the value of narratives over mobile distractions.

By embracing **interactive storytelling**, children/ students and adults can explore their creativity, enhance their communication skills and build meaningful connections, all while stepping away from mobile devices. This approach encourages active participation in storytelling, fostering a love for narratives that can lead to healthier habits and more enriching interactions.

|| ॐ ||

20

Side Effects of Mobile Addiction

'Mobile Addiction' goes beyond just a decrease in productivity; it can have far-reaching effects on both mental and physical health. This chapter delves into the side effects of excessive mobile use, shedding light on how constant screen time can disrupt sleep patterns, lead to anxiety, affect attention span and even cause long-term damage to relationships. The impact isn't limited to adults–children too, are increasingly vulnerable to these side effects. By understanding the various consequences of mobile addiction, we can better appreciate the need for balanced screen time and take steps to mitigate its negative effects. This chapter offers a closer look at how mobile overuse affects our well-being and provides strategies to protect ourselves from these harmful side effects.

'Mobile Addiction' can have a range of side effects on children/ students/ adults, impacting their physical health, mental well-being and social skills. Here are some of the key side effects:

1. Physical Health Issues:

a). **Eye Strain and Vision Problems:** Prolonged screen time can lead to eye strain, blurred vision and even near sightedness (myopia) due to constant close-up screen viewing.

b). **Poor Posture:** Continuous use of mobile devices often results in poor posture, leading to neck and back pain (sometimes referred to as "text neck").

c). Sleep Disturbances: Exposure to blue light from screens can disrupt the body's natural sleep-wake cycle, making it harder for children to fall asleep and stay asleep.

2. Cognitive and Mental Health Effects:

a). Reduced Attention Span: Frequent device usage and constant switching between apps can reduce a child's ability to focus and lead to shorter attention spans.

b). Impaired Memory: Relying on devices can impact memory retention and cognitive skills, as children may become less inclined to retain information without digital prompts.

c). Increased Anxiety and Stress: Excessive screen time can lead to overstimulation, which can cause feelings of anxiety, stress and irritability, particularly if they're exposed to negative content.

3. Emotional and Social Development Challenges:

a). Social Isolation: Children who spend excessive time on mobile devices may miss out on real-life social interactions, leading to isolation and difficulty developing social skills.

b). Emotional Regulation Issues: Mobile addiction may make it difficult for children to manage emotions, as they may seek screens to distract themselves or cope, which can limit their resilience.

c). Dependency and Withdrawal Symptoms: When children are restricted from device use, they may display withdrawal symptoms like mood swings, anger or sadness.

4. Behavioural Issues:

a). Decreased Interest in Outdoor Activities: Mobile addiction can replace physical play and outdoor activities, which are crucial for healthy development.

b). **Impulse Control Problems:** Engaging in instant gratification activities on devices can make it harder for children to exercise patience and control their impulses.

c). **Aggressive Behaviour:** Overexposure to violent or fast-paced content can increase aggression or impatience in children.

5. Impact on Academic Performance:

a). **Decline in Academic Focus:** Mobile addiction can lead to a lack of interest in academics and studying, impacting grades and academic achievements.

b). **Reduced Creativity:** Relying on pre-made content can stifle creativity, as children may engage less in imaginative play or problem-solving activities.

6. Developmental Delays in Younger Children:

a). **Delayed Language and Social Skills:** In very young children, excessive screen time can slow the development of language and social interaction skills due to a lack of verbal and physical play.

b). **Delayed Motor Skills:** Mobile devices often don't require fine motor skills like traditional toys do, which can impact dexterity and coordination in younger children.

7. Exposure to Inappropriate Content:

a). **Unsupervised Access:** Mobile addiction increases the risk of children/ students coming across inappropriate or harmful content online, which can negatively impact their mental and emotional development.

These effects underscore the importance of managing screen time and guiding children/ students towards healthier, balanced use of mobile devices.

|| ॐ ||

21

Shaping Tomorrow

The choices we make today shape the future, we live tomorrow.

In a world where mobile technology influences almost every aspect of our lives, it's crucial to guide the next generation towards responsible use. This chapter explores how fostering mindful mobile habits today can lead to healthier, more balanced lives in the future. By prioritizing meaningful connections, personal growth and digital well-being, we can influence not just our own futures but also the future of society. 'Shaping Tomorrow' provides practical insights on how to nurture a mind-full relationship with technology, ensuring that mobile devices remain a tool for progress, rather than a source of harm.

If a society becomes widely addicted to mobile devices without a balance, the long-term impacts could reshape the country's future in significant ways. Here are some potential consequences:

1. Decline in Physical and Mental Health:

a). **Public Health Crisis:** Widespread mobile addiction could increase health problems like obesity, eye disorders, poor posture and mental health issues, placing strain on healthcare systems and resources.

b). **Higher Rates of Anxiety and Depression:** With more people using screens as an emotional escape, mental health issues like anxiety, depression and loneliness could rise, affecting productivity and quality of life.

2. Reduced Productivity and Economic Impact:

a). **Loss in Workplace Productivity:** Constant distraction by mobile devices in the workplace could reduce productivity, innovation and efficiency, impacting the economy.

b). **Decreased Workforce Skills:** An overreliance on devices may reduce problem-solving and creativity skills, as well as critical thinking, which are crucial for economic growth and technological advancement.

c). **Innovation Stagnation:** With reduced face-to-face collaboration, brainstorming and hands-on problem-solving, creative innovation could suffer.

3. Weakening of Social and Family Bonds:

a). **Erosion of Family Values and Social Skills:** Excessive screen time often replaces real-life interaction, potentially weakening family relationships and leading to a society less capable of healthy social bonding.

b). **Social Isolation and Reduced Empathy:** People may become increasingly isolated or develop shallow relationships online, leading to reduced empathy, compassion and understanding within communities.

4. Educational and Cognitive Decline:

a). **Reduced Academic Performance:** For children and students, excessive screen time can disrupt learning, reducing focus, comprehension and critical thinking, which can lead to long-term educational setbacks.

b). **Dependency on Technology:** A reliance on devices for information and memory can hinder cognitive abilities with younger generations potentially facing challenges in retaining knowledge and problem-solving independently.

5. Loss of Cultural and Traditional Values:

a). **Dilution of Cultural Heritage:** With increased screen time replacing cultural practices, people may lose interest in traditional activities, languages and values, leading to an erosion of cultural identity.

b). **Shift from Outdoor Recreation:** A reduction in community gatherings, festivals and nature activities may result in people becoming more disconnected from their environment and cultural roots.

6. Impact on National Security and Awareness:

a). **Vulnerability to Cyber Security Risks:** Increased mobile usage makes people more exposed to cyber security threats, misinformation and manipulation, which can have national security implications.

b). **Decrease in Civic Engagement:** With excessive screen time, there may be reduced participation in civic responsibilities like voting, volunteering and community activities, weakening democratic processes and social cohesion.

7. Environmental Impact:

a). **e-Waste and Pollution:** With increasing reliance on mobile devices comes more frequent device replacement, contributing to electronic waste and environmental pollution.

b). **Increased Carbon Footprint:** The energy demand for digital devices, cloud storage and data centres will rise, potentially increasing the carbon footprint and accelerating climate change.

8. Shift in Economic Landscape:

a). **Dependence on Tech Industries:** With more focus on technology, traditional industries may decline, reducing the diversity of job opportunities and economic resilience.

b). **Transformation in Consumer Habits:** An addiction-driven economy may fuel consumerism and instant gratification, which can create unsustainable demands and resource depletion.

9. Potential for Innovation in Mental Health Solutions:

a). **Increased Demand for Mindfulness and Rehabilitation:** A positive outcome could be an innovation in mental health solutions and digital wellness. This could encourage research and resources into mental well-being and balance.

10. Opportunity for a Shift to Digital Well-being Policies:

a). **National Emphasis on Digital Literacy:** Governments may prioritize digital literacy, teaching citizens about healthy device use and digital boundaries.

b). **Stronger Regulations and Policies:** Recognizing the impact of mobile addiction, governments might implement policies to control excessive digital marketing to children, ensuring platforms encourage healthier usage.

The future of a society overly reliant on mobile devices could hinge on whether steps are taken now to educate, set boundaries and foster a balanced approach to technology. Integrating digital well-being into our lives can help preserve health, culture and productivity while enabling us to benefit from the advancements that technology offers.

Consistency and communication are the keys when implementing these techniques. It's important to create a supportive and understanding environment as children adjust to reduced screen time. Additionally, involving children in the decision-making process and explaining the rationale behind these techniques can help them feel more invested in making positive changes.

Remember that each child is unique, so it's important to tailor these techniques to their individual personalities and needs. Additionally, fostering a positive and supportive environment is the key to successfully reducing mobile addiction and encouraging healthier habits.

We think it can help all the parents to remove mobile addiction in your child as well as in your daily routine. By the help of these points, anyone can remove mobile addiction and live a beautiful life which can connect you with the nature and your own family. Try this and please reply as you achieve the critical changes in your life.

22

Mobile Addiction and Numerology

How Birth Numbers Reflect Tendencies and Habits

Mobile addiction can stem from personality traits, habits and daily challenges. Numerology, the universal divine science and cosmic language of numbers, through Birth Numbers (1 to 9), provides insights into the tendencies, traits and habits that may lead to mobile dependency. Each Birth Number has unique characteristics influencing its relationship with technology and personalized strategies to overcome 'Mobile Addiction'.

Birth Number: 1, Leader/ Innovator

Born on the dates – 1, 10, 19 or 28 of any month

- **Tendencies: Driven and Goal-oriented**, they may overuse mobile phones for work-related tasks, leadership management and innovative tasks or to stay informed. Their addiction often arises from constant tracking of performance or achievements.
- **Challenges:** Overworking, stress and difficulty disconnecting from tasks.
- **Advice:** Set structured phone usage times for work and leisure. Delegate responsibilities to reduce reliance on mobile devices. Engage in hobbies that promote creativity and relaxation.

Birth Number: 2, Diplomatic/ Emotional

Born on the dates – 2, 11, 20 or 29 of any month

- **Tendencies: Emotional and Relationship-focused**, they often use mobile phones for communication and validation. They may get addicted to messaging, social media or apps that facilitate connections.

- **Challenges:** Difficulty detaching from relationships and feeling emotionally dependent on digital interactions.
- **Advice:** Create boundaries for phone use during specific hours. Prioritize face-to-face communication to build emotional resilience and avoid excessive texting or scrolling.

Birth Number: 3, Communicator/ Consultant

Born on the dates – 3, 12, 21 or 30 of any month

- **Tendencies: Fun-Loving and Social**, they may become addicted to entertainment apps, games or social platforms to stay connected and entertained.
- **Challenges:** Procrastination, escapism and avoidance of routine tasks.
- **Advice:** Schedule dedicated times for mobile use and balance it with offline creative activities like writing or painting. Set achievable daily goals to maintain focus on priorities.

Birth Number: 4, Organizer/ Disciplined

Born on the dates – 4, 13, 22 or 31 of any month

- **Tendencies: Disciplined and Methodical**, they may overuse productivity apps, online shopping, news and glamour/ fashion world or information-based platforms. Their addiction arises from a desire for order and routine.
- **Challenges:** Rigidity in routines and excessive planning or data consumption.
- **Advice:** Limit app use by substituting digital tools with offline planners or physical books. Practice flexibility by introducing spontaneous, phone-free activities into your daily life.

Birth Number: 5, Adventurer/ Resourceful

Born on the dates – 5, 14 or 23 of any month

- **Tendencies: Curious and Thrill-seeking**, they may use mobile phones excessively for entertainment, fast-paced communication and path finding or exploration through social media, games or travel blogs.
- **Challenges:** Restlessness, impatience and seeking instant gratification.
- **Advice:** Use technology intentionally by dedicating specific time slots for exploration. Channel your energy into physical activities or hobbies like sports to reduce screen time.

Birth Number: 6, Nurturer/ Care-taker

Born on the dates – 6, 15 or 24 of any month

- **Tendencies: Compassionate and Responsible**, they might overuse mobile phones to maintain relationships, check on loved and the dearest ones or find comfort through digital interactions.
- **Challenges:** Over-involvement in others' lives and difficulty prioritizing personal time.
- **Advice:** Set clear limits for digital communication. Focus on self-care practices and use physical activities to recharge emotionally without relying on a device.

Birth Number: 7, Seeker/ Secretive

Born on the dates – 7, 16 or 25 of any month

- **Tendencies: Introspective and Analytical**, they may use mobile phones excessively for research, seeking and increasing knowledge or spiritual exploration.
- **Challenges:** Isolation, overthinking and detachment from social reality.

- **Advice:** Dedicate specific time slots for learning and balance it with real-life applications of knowledge. Take phone-free walks or practice mindfulness to reconnect with the physical world.

Birth Number: 8, Achiever/ Hard-worker

Born on the dates – 8, 17 or 26 of any month

- **Tendencies: Ambitious and Success-driven**, they often use mobile phones for work-related tasks, financial tracking or staying ahead of the competition.
- **Challenges:** Stress, workaholic and difficulty switching off from professional responsibilities.
- **Advice:** Set boundaries for phone use after work hours. Practice relaxation techniques like meditation and focus on non-material aspects of life for fulfillment.

Birth Number: 9, Humanitarian/ Helpful

Born on the dates – 9, 18 or 27 of any month

- **Tendencies: Passionate and Empathetic**, they may overuse mobile phones to stay connected with causes or help others through social platforms or messaging apps.
- **Challenges:** Emotional burnout, over-involvement in advocacy or escapism through digital means.
- **Advice:** Balance digital advocacy with hands-on activities for causes. Schedule tech-free time to recharge emotionally and engage in self-care practices.

Important Tips and Take Away for Managing 'Mobile Addiction'

1). **Digital Detox:** Incorporate regular breaks from technology into your routine.

2). **Mindful Usage:** Be conscious of your triggers and usage patterns.

3). **Healthy Alternatives:** Replace screen time with hobbies, outdoor activities, or social interactions.

4). **Self-Discipline:** Use apps to track usage and set daily limits.

5). **Gratitude Practice:** Focus on offline relationships and experiences to find fulfillment beyond the screen.

Numerology provides a personalized lens to understand and manage 'Mobile Addiction', guiding individuals to maintain balance in their lives. If you'd like a deeper analysis or specific recommendations feel free to connect with us by sending an e-mail!!!

|| ॐ ||

23

Pledge(s)

**Pledge(s) to Protect
Yourself and Next Generation
From
Mobile Addiction**

The pledge serves as a powerful commitment, empowering parents to take proactive steps in protecting their children and students as well as adults from 'Mobile Addiction', fostering accountability and strengthening family bonds through shared responsibility and healthier habits.

|| ॐ ||

E-mail : ankakshrmiracless@gmail.com
Whatsapp # +91-9368746306

My Pledge Against Mobile Addiction

(Child/ Student/ Adult/ Reader)

I, ………… ………… ………… ………… ………… <*name*>, acknowledge the impact of excessive mobile use on my personal well-being, relationships and productivity. I am committed to breaking free from the grip of 'Mobile Addiction' and regaining control over my time and focus.

I really pledge to:

1. Apply the techniques and strategies outlined in this book to reduce my dependency on mobile devices.
2. Set boundaries for my mobile usage to prioritize real-life interactions and activities.
3. Be mindful of the time I spend on screens and strive for a healthier digital balance.
4. Encourage others around me to adopt mindful mobile habits and create a supportive environment.
5. Hold myself accountable to make a positive change for my mental, emotional and social well-being.

By taking this pledge, I choose to reclaim my time, rediscover my potential and inspire others to do the same. Together, we can combat 'Mobile Addiction' and lead more fulfilling lives.

Signature: _____________________   **Date:** _______________

E-mail ID: _____________________   **Mobile:** _______________

Name and complete address:

____

____

____

"The Authors' request to take this pledge to make a difference in your life and others' lives!"

My Pledge Against Mobile Addiction

(Father/ Mother/ Teacher/ Consultant)

I, ... *<as parent/ teacher/ consultant/ doctor/ other* ....> I recognize the harmful effects of excessive mobile use on my child's/ client's/ student's/ patient's physical, mental and emotional well-being. I am committed to guiding him toward healthier habits and fostering a balanced lifestyle.

I really pledge to:

1. **Understand and Implement** the techniques shared in this book to reduce his/ her dependency on mobile devices.
2. **Lead by Example**, demonstrating mindful mobile usage in my own life.
3. **Establish Boundaries** for mobile use in our home, promoting quality family time and engaging activities.
4. **Encourage Outdoor Play and Creative Pursuits**, offering my child alternatives to screen-based entertainment.
5. **Communicate and Educate** my child about the benefits of controlled mobile usage and the potential harms of addiction.
6. **Stay Consistent and Patient**, supporting his/ her journey toward freedom from 'Mobile Addiction'.

By taking this pledge, I promise to prioritize my child's/ client's/ student's/ patient's overall well-being and actively contribute to shaping a healthier, more focused future for them. Together, as a family/ consultant/ advisor, we will combat 'Mobile Addiction' and embrace a life filled with meaningful connections and experiences.

Signature: ___________________   Date: ________________

E-mail ID: ___________________   Mobile: _______________

Name and complete address:

____

____

____

"The Authors' request to take this pledge to make a difference in your life and others' lives!"

My Pledge to Spread Awareness and Help Others Combat
'Mobile Addiction'

(Anyone)

I, ………… ………… ………… ………… ………… ………… *<name>*, having benefited from the insights and techniques shared in this book, pledge to extend this positive change to others and contribute to building a healthier, mobile-balanced society.

I really pledge to:

1. **Introduce This Book** to at least three individuals/ parents/ family, friends or colleagues—who may be struggling with 'Mobile Addiction' or seeking healthier habits.
2. **Support Others** by actively discussing the techniques in the book, guiding them on how to apply these methods in their lives.
3. **Inspire a Movement**, encouraging those I help to pass on this knowledge to others, creating a chain of positive influence.
4. **Leverage My Networks**—social media, community groups or personal circles—to promote the message of mindful mobile usage and share my journey.
5. **Champion Responsible Mobile Use**, ensuring the wisdom of this book reaches not just individuals, but families and communities, fostering long-term change.

Through this pledge, I commit to being a beacon of awareness and support, empowering others to reclaim their time, focus and relationships from the clutches of 'Mobile Addiction'. Together, we can transform lives, one step at a time.

Signature: _________________   Date: _________________

E-mail ID: _________________   Mobile: _________________

Name and complete address:

____

____

____

"The Authors' request to take this pledge to make a difference in your life and others' lives!"

|| ॐ ||

Blurb

Teachers and Parents should collaborate to set clear guidelines for responsible usage of mobile and other electronic devices, including appropriate times for usage, content restrictions and balance between screen time and other activities.

We can't remove the **Mobile Phone** from your hands, because of its importance, but can handle it's time limit for maintaining the health as well as our child's future.

Certainly, 21 simple, but important techniques to remove or reduce **"Mobile Addiction in Children/ Students and Adults"**, have been shared in this book.

List of Books

Books written by Abhishaik Chitraans:

1. **Sex**: A Complex Intersection of Physical Need and Mental Well-being
2. **Life**: A Dance of Light and Shadow
3. **The God's Tender**: Love & Care
4. **Mobile Addiction**: 21 Simple Techniques to remove or reduce Mobile Addiction in Children and Adults
5. **P³**: The Triple Power of Alphabet–P (Proud, Pain, Prayer)

Books written by Rainu Mangtani:

1. **The Height of Life in 24 Rains**: An Inspirational Auto Biography
2. **Today's Corporate World**: A Robotic Mechanism of Youth
3. **Ladder of Success**: Best 15 Ways to Achieve Your Goals

i. **Deep Secrets of Name** : A comprehensive book on advanced Name Numerology based on Chaldean System & an extensive research based on real life case studies. The best book on Name Numerology by 3 eminent Indian authors in Google search, launched at Pragati Maidan, New Delhi in World Book Fair 2024.

   Mr. Abhishaik Chitraans is as main Author/ Guide of the book with the two renowned authors and research scholars of Numerology namely Mrs. Rainu Mangtani (Numerologist & Graphologist) and Mrs. Jyotsnaa G Bansal (Astro-Numerologist).

ii. **Women Empowerment and Economic Developments** : An anthology/ articles collection of 51 Co-Authors, lunched on occasion of International Women's Day and Mahashivratri, 08th March, 2024 with online presence of Padma Shri recipient Smt. Gulabo Sapera ji, a legendary folk artist.

Other upcoming Books :

iii. **My Marriage : Bliss vs Curse**
(Anthology of 108 eminent Co-authors)

iv. **Seven LEE of Life**
(Anthology of 108 visionary Co-authors)

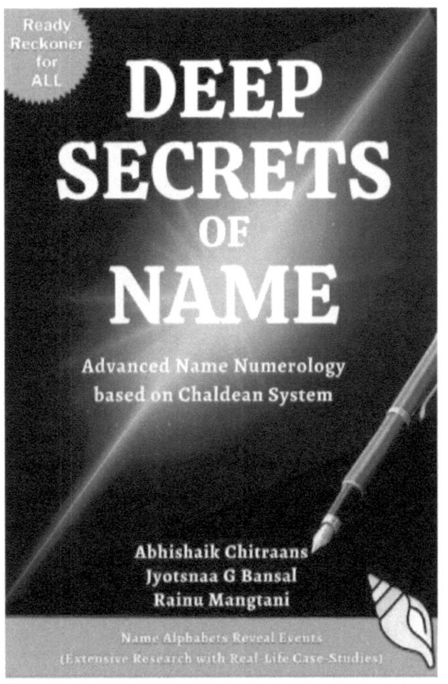
Ready Reckoner for ALL
DEEP SECRETS OF NAME
Advanced Name Numerology based on Chaldean System
Abhishaik Chitraans
Jyotsnaa G Bansal
Rainu Mangtani
Name Alphabets Reveal Events
(Extensive Research with Real-Life Case-Studies)

Women Empowerment and Economic Developments
Anthology of 51 Co-Authors
Compiled by
Rainu Mangtani • Abhishaik Chitraans
Jyotsnaa G Bansal

Seven LEE of Life
Anthology of Wisdom by 108 Visionaries
Learning
Earning   Expectation
Compiled by
ABHISHAIK CHITRAANS
RAINU MANGTANI

My Marriage
Bliss vs Curse
An Anthology of 108 Co-Authors
Compiled by
ABHISHAIK CHITRAANS | RAINU MANGTANI

शब्दों का समंदर है यह,
बस डूबकर पढ़ते जाना है।
इंतजार करो किताब का अगली,
हमें काफिला बड़ा बनाना है॥

रेनू – अभिषेक

E-mail : ankakshrmiracless@gmail.com
Whatsapp # +91-9368746306